EZINE KALEIDOSCOPE FEBRUARY 2025

NAVIGATING RELATIONSHIPS

EZINE KALEIDOSCOPE

Contents

CREDITS

Volume 1 Issue 5 2025

Founder/Editor: Meetu Sehgal

Associate Editor: Chahat Singh

Cover Design: Tony and Priya Gupta

Graphic Design: Dilip Kumar

Digital Media Marketing: Raza Kamil

Project and Growth Catalyst: Yash Yadav

Business and Market Strategy: Ashi Sharma

Legal Advisor: Arushi Sharma

Owned by Meetu Sehgal

at S-423, Greater Kailash-I, New Delhi – 110048

Published by Notion Press

Contact Information

M: +91 9953753637

E: info@ezinekaleidoscope.com

W: www.EzineKaleidoscope.com

From The Editor's Desk

Dear Reader,

Welcome to the February 2025 edition of *Ezine Kaleidoscope*. This month, we explore a theme that weaves its way through every facet of our lives: **Navigating Relationships**. From the bonds of love and friendship to the intricate dance of trust and connection, relationships shape us, challenge us, and often teach us more about ourselves than we expect.

Relationships are the most intimate and important aspect of our lives. However, navigating them can feel like walking in the dark, not knowing what to expect next, having no idea of how to deal with the emotions and connections that bind us and how to sustain them so they stay healthy.

When relationships hit turbulent waters, they need to be rescued and healed. But more than this, it is also imperative that one looks within to see what within us perhaps caused the turbulence. Some questions that can help you understand this are:

- Who am I in this relationship today?
- How am I showing up here in this moment?
- What are my emotions or underlying thoughts and feelings in the present?
- Is there anything that is causing me to feel insecure, disrespected or frustrated?
- If so, have I worked on my emotions?
- Have I spoken to my partner to resolve what is happening or am I blaming them for it all?

Self-reflection is a powerful tool, whether you are looking for spiritual development or to create a healthy, long-lasting relationship. Above are a few questions that can begin your journey into looking within to know your role in relationship problems.

An important thing that we often forget is that a relationship requires two individuals – with their unique identities, qualities, desires and perspectives. A relationship takes two to tango. One partner's self-reflection can sometimes help save the relationship, but in the long run, both partners need to be willing to help improve their bond and create a healthy connection.

A few important things in a healthy relationship include **Respect, Authenticity, Connection, and Safety**. Respect allows individuals to honour each other's boundaries and individuality. Authenticity fosters trust and genuine connections. True connection builds a sense of togetherness, and safety creates a foundation where vulnerability and growth can flourish.

In this edition, we have curated a collection of articles that delve into the complexities, joys, and lessons of relationships. Each piece offers unique insights and practical wisdom to help you deepen your connections and better understand the dynamics at play.

You will journey into the psychology of love and understand attachment styles – how individuals with different upbringings show up in relationships, the allure of bad boys and how to handle mismatched expectations. You will also find actionable strategies to nurture relationships that are fulfilling and free of unnecessary drama. Modern relationships for GenZs can be confusing, therefore you will find insights into understanding the modern complexities of relationships and much more.

As you read through this edition, we invite you to reflect on your own relationships. What do they teach you about yourself? How can you nurture them further? Whether it's through understanding psychology, embracing spirituality, or simply sharing a meal, relationships are a mirror of our inner world.

We would love to read about your insights and reflections that this edition sparked for you. Do share your feedback on social media or through an email at info@EzineKaleidoscope.com.

Light and Grace

Meetu Sehgal
Founder and Editor-in-Chief
Trainer, Therapist, Tarot Reader and Psychologist

I

The Sacred Art of Navigating Relationships: Building Deeper Connections and Emotional Harmony

The Sacred Art of Relationships:
Building Emotional Harmony and
Soulful Connections

The Sacred Art of Navigating Relationships: Building Deeper Connections and Emotional Harmony

Relationships are the foundation of human existence. They influence our emotional well-being, spiritual growth, and sense of purpose. Whether it's the bond with a partner, family member, friend, or colleague, every relationship offers an opportunity to grow, heal, and connect on a soul level. Yet, navigating relationships in today's fast-paced, modern world can be challenging. Expectations, misunderstandings, and unhealed wounds can create distance, making it difficult to maintain the emotional harmony we desire.

This article explores the sacred art of navigating relationships, emphasizing the importance of communication, self-awareness, and spiritual connection. Whether you're seeking to heal a strained bond, deepen your existing connections, or attract healthier relationships into your life, these insights will guide you on this transformative journey.

Understanding the Spiritual Purpose of Relationships

Relationships are more than just social constructs—they are spiritual tools for growth. Every interaction carries a lesson, whether it's about love, patience, forgiveness, or understanding. When viewed from a spiritual perspective, even challenging relationships serve a purpose. They mirror our own unhealed wounds, teaching us to look inward and address the areas where we need growth.

- **Soul Contracts:** In spiritual teachings, it is believed that before birth, our souls create agreements with others to meet and learn specific lessons. Recognizing this can help us approach relationships with greater compassion and understanding.
- **Reflection and Growth:** Relationships act as mirrors. If you're experiencing conflict, it may be reflecting something within yourself that needs healing. Ask yourself: What is this relationship teaching me?

The Role of Self-Awareness in Relationships

Healthy relationships begin with self-awareness. Before you can truly connect with others, you need to connect with yourself. Knowing your values, boundaries, and emotional triggers lays the foundation for meaningful connections.

1. **Practice Self-Love:** When you value yourself, you set the standard for how others should treat you. Self-love is not selfish; it's a necessity for healthy relationships.
2. **Understand Your Triggers:** Reflect on past conflicts. What patterns do you notice? Understanding your triggers helps you respond consciously instead of reacting impulsively.
3. **Set Boundaries:** Clear boundaries protect your energy and foster mutual respect. Communicate with them lovingly but firmly.

Communication: The Bridge to Connection

Effective communication is the cornerstone of any strong relationship. Without it, misunderstandings and resentments can grow, creating distance.

- **Listen to Understand, Not Respond:** Many people listen with the intent to reply rather than truly understanding the other person's perspective. Practice active listening by giving your full attention and acknowledging their feelings.
- **Speak from the Heart:** When expressing your feelings, use "I" statements instead of "you" statements. For example, say, "I feel hurt when…" instead of "You always make me feel…". This approach minimizes defensiveness.
- **Embrace Silence:** Not all communication is verbal. Sometimes, holding space for someone in silence speaks louder than words.

Healing Emotional Wounds in Relationships

Unhealed emotional wounds can create barriers to intimacy and trust. Whether these wounds stem from childhood experiences or past relationships, they can influence how you interact with others. Healing these wounds is essential for cultivating healthier connections.

1. **Acknowledge the Pain:** Suppressing emotions only prolongs the healing process. Acknowledge your pain and give yourself the permission to feel

it.

2. **Seek Forgiveness:** Forgiveness doesn't mean condoning harmful behaviour—it means releasing emotional weight. Forgive others and yourself to free your heart from resentment.

3. **Practice Inner Child Healing:** Many of our relational patterns are rooted in childhood experiences. Nurture your inner child by offering the love and validation you may not have received.

Building Emotional Intimacy

Emotional intimacy is the glue that holds relationships together. It's about creating a safe space where both individuals feel seen, heard, and valued.

- **Vulnerability as Strength:** True intimacy requires vulnerability. Share your fears, dreams, and insecurities. When you open up, it invites others to do the same.
- **Practice Gratitude:** Express appreciation for your loved ones regularly. A simple "thank you" can go a long way in strengthening bonds.
- **Create Rituals Together:** Whether it's a weekly check-in, a morning coffee ritual, or a shared meditation practice, rituals foster connection and consistency.

Navigating Conflicts with Grace

Conflict is inevitable in any relationship, but it doesn't have to be destructive. When approached with mindfulness and respect, conflict can lead to deeper understanding and growth.

1. **Pause Before Reacting:** When emotions run high, take a moment to breathe and collect your thoughts. Responding mindfully prevents unnecessary escalation.
2. **Focus on Solutions, Not Blame:** Shift the focus from who's at fault to how you can resolve the issue together. This collaborative approach fosters teamwork.
3. **Agree to Disagree:** It's okay to have different perspectives. Respect each other's views and find common ground.

The Role of Energy in Relationships

Every relationship carries an energetic exchange. If you feel drained or overwhelmed after interacting with someone, it's a sign that the energy is unbalanced.

- **Protect Your Energy:** Practice energy-clearing techniques, such as visualization, grounding, or meditation, to release negativity.
- **Surround Yourself with Positivity:** Choose relationships that uplift and inspire you. Let go of toxic connections that no longer serve your highest good.
- **Raise Your Vibration:** Engage in activities that bring you joy and peace. The higher your vibration, the more positive relationships you'll attract.

Attracting Healthy Relationships

If you're seeking new relationships, whether romantic or platonic, the energy you project plays a significant role. Like attracts like. By embodying the qualities you desire in others, you'll naturally attract similar energy.

1. **Visualize Your Ideal Connection:** Spend time visualizing the type of relationship you want. Focus on the feelings it brings, rather than the specific details.
2. **Be Open to Possibilities:** Release rigid expectations and trust that the Universe will bring the right people into your life at the right time.
3. **Take Inspired Action:** Join communities, attend events, or engage in activities aligned with your values to meet like-minded individuals.

The Spiritual Connection in Relationships

A spiritually connected relationship transcends the physical and emotional realms. It's about aligning with each other's souls and growing together on your spiritual paths.

- **Meditate Together:** Shared meditation deepens your connection and aligns your energies.
- **Practice Mindful Presence:** Be fully present with your loved ones. Put away distractions and give them your undivided attention.
- **Support Each Other's Growth:** Encourage your loved ones to pursue their passions and spiritual journeys, even if they differ from your own.

The Journey Within: A Relationship with Yourself

The most important relationship you'll ever have is the one with yourself. When you nurture this connection, all other relationships naturally flourish.

1. **Embrace Solitude:** Spend time alone to reflect, recharge, and connect with your inner self.
2. **Practice Self-Compassion:** Treat yourself with the same kindness and understanding you offer others.
3. **Align with Your Higher Self:** Regularly tune into your intuition and spiritual practices to stay aligned with your true essence.

Final Thoughts: Relationships as Sacred Journeys

Navigating relationships is both an art and a journey. Each connection, whether fleeting or lifelong, offers a sacred opportunity to grow, heal, and love. By approaching relationships with self-awareness, compassion, and spiritual mindfulness, you can create deeper bonds and experience the joy of authentic connection.

Remember, every relationship begins with you. When you cultivate love, understanding, and harmony within yourself, it reflects in all your connections. So, take a deep breath, embrace the lessons, and trust in the beautiful journey of navigating relationships.

About the Writer

Bhawna Berry

Bhawna is a gifted intuitive and mystic with a lifelong connection to the spiritual realm. From a young age, she demonstrated a unique sensitivity to energies and a natural ability to distinguish clarity from confusion, a gift her family recognized early on. With a postgraduate degree and a thriving professional career, Bhawna followed her true calling to support others, using her intuitive insights and spiritual tools to guide people through life's challenges. Known by some as a prodigy in the mystical arts, Bhawna's journey has led her to explore diverse spiritual tools and practices, from Energy Aura Reading to Akashic Records Reading, Tarot, Chakra balancing, and Rune interpretation. She also deeply understands the Law of Attraction and how it can empower and transform lives. She uses these tools now to help others find peace and purpose by bringing light to their shadowed paths and transforming negative situations into growth opportunities.

II

Love Without the Chaos: 5 Rules for Effortless Relationships

Love Without the Chaos:
5 Rules for Effortless Relationships

Relationships can feel like you're constantly navigating a minefield of emotions. We look for fulfilling relationships and connections, but often what follows is frustrations, disappointments and a messy affair. This can make one feel like relationships are too complicated to handle.

In my career of guiding clients through their relationships, I have found that often it is not the relationship that is complicated, but our expectations, desires and lack of self-awareness that complicates things.

What if I told you that navigating the world of relationships doesn't have to be a constant uphill battle? Through years of helping clients in their own relationship journeys, and with a healthy dose of self-reflection on my own, I've distilled some key "rules" that can significantly simplify this often-complex area of life. These aren't strict commandments but rather guiding principles designed to nurture healthier, happier, and more fulfilling connections.

So, buckle up and get ready to ditch the chaos and embrace a more effortless approach to love.

Think of these rules as your relationship GPS, or perhaps as an angel sitting on your shoulder whispering some guidance in your ear. They're not about controlling others or manipulating or forcing things to be a certain way. Instead, they focus on cultivating self-awareness, fostering open communication, and prioritizing your own well-being within the context of your partnership.

Whether you're seeking a new romance, looking to revitalize an existing one, or simply wanting to understand yourself better in the realm of relationships, these rules offer valuable insights and practical strategies to help you create connections that are both meaningful and enjoyable.

Rule No.1: Say What You Mean - Communicate

Duh! Isn't that what we do? Well, you will be surprised how often it is not the case. This is especially true if you are a people pleaser.

Here is how to keep things simple:

Want attention? Ask for it.

Want a hug? Ask for it.

Want a cup of coffee? Make one for yourself and one for your partner too! Or ask for it.

Want to tell them what you like? Say it plainly.

Want to let them know what you don't like? Umm... say it too.

If you are expecting your partner to read between the lines, if you are expecting them to understand your needs or meanings without you saying it clearly, you are setting your relationship up for some major drama. Unless your partner is a psychic (even if they are), please spell it clearly whatever you want and what you mean.

Make it easy for the other person to connect to you. No one wants to solve puzzles day in and day out with someone they want to feel safe with.

Yes, relationships are meant to be a safe space. If you are not feeling safe, say so. If your partner is not feeling safe enough to be themselves, this needs to be addressed with some loving communication.

Therapist's interpretation: Being unable to express yourself clearly can indicate fear of judgment and criticism underneath. If, on reflection, this is what you feel is happening, please address this with your therapist. And no, your partner isn't your therapist. They can support you in your healing journey, but they may not be qualified enough or unbiased enough to help you through this.

Also, if you expect your partner to just know what you want or mean because that is how you will feel loved, then you are bound to be disappointed at some point (or more points) in your relationship. Perhaps this is your love language, but this is not healthy for you or your partner. Communicate.

Rule No.2: Listen Deeply Before Replying

Listening is an underrated skill. We are hearing all the time, but are we really listening?

When one speaks, their body language conveys more than their words can ever. So listening also means paying attention to their whole being to really understand what they are trying to communicate.

When you listen to your partner, pay attention to their words, tone, and body language.

- Practice active listening. This means you are not just listening to reply to them; you are listening to understand.
- Ask meaningful questions to help you understand better.
- Ask your partner if they are venting or sharing or if they are looking for feedback.

When you listen deeply, you will get to know more about your partner as well, how they see the world, what emotions are going through them and what they might need at the moment.

This is the kind of work that a relationship needs - being present.

Therapist's interpretation: We are all looking at the world through our lenses made of our personal histories, beliefs and desires. We see what we really want to see. Rarely do we see the reality. This is also what is happening when we listen.

If you were to pause and really notice what happens the moment you listen to someone, you will be surprised to know that many of the times, you are not even present for the whole conversation. You have drifted off in your head, making internal connections based on what you hear, picking up on words that sound familiar. A whole different conversation is happening inside your head. Many conclusions have already happened based on what little you heard. You have been mentally absent. Meanwhile, you have missed what your partner really wants to communicate. This is the root of many miscommunications.

Make an effort to listen as if this is the first time you are meeting your partner and are really interested in knowing what they have to say.

Rule No.3: When Triggered, Deal With It First, Then Talk

Remember that time when you felt frustrated with something at work or what your partner said, and you lashed out at them, dragging the past in the way, thinking or assuming that it was your partner's fault that you felt something?

The truth is, they just happened to probably trigger an already underlying emotion within you. But it was your emotion in the first place, hence it is your job to deal with it.

Often, we place the burden of our emotions on others, especially our partners or family. This is the biggest reason why many relationships become sour and lose their sweetness.

If you have to communicate something, please deal with your emotions first, then talk. That communication will be more constructive than an angry rant or an argument.

Therapist's interpretation: Emotions are a powerful force that can lead you to destroy the best of relationships, if not handled well. Remember, if you are feeling an emotion, it is not because of somebody. That somebody may have triggered it, but the cause of that emotion has been within you.

An emotion could be triggered because you feel judged, dismissed, frustrated, insecure or afraid deep within. If the root of that emotion is healed, if the root is not there, no one can trigger that emotional response in you.

Being triggered by someone means you have handed them complete responsibility for your emotions. Essentially, you are saying, "I am not responsible for how I behave or feel, you are!!"

Relationships need work, yes. That work involves taking responsibility for your emotions and trauma and healing them. Your family or loved ones don't have to suffer your trauma responses.

Rule No.4: Learn To Respect Boundaries—Yours And Theirs

Boundaries are important in relationships. Boundaries define where you begin and where you end. A relationship is between two people who are individuals, with their own set of beliefs, perspectives and choices. If one of the persons doesn't have a clearly defined boundary, it's almost like they don't even exist in the relationship.

Boundaries help with an important aspect in a relationship, perhaps the most important quality - Respect.

If you feel disrespected in your relationship, check to see if you respect yourself enough, if you have clear boundaries or not.

This is what goes wrong with people pleasers and those who change or sacrifice themselves in relationships completely. If you choose to only exist for others, you are essentially telling the world (including your partner) that your needs are not important and that you don't exist. In such a case, chances are, your needs will go unmet or unseen by your partner causing you to feel even more hurt and disappointed.

Boundaries are defined by what you tolerate and what you don't. Just as your skin is your physical boundary, your aura is your energetic boundary, similarly, your choices and what you tolerate are your boundary, or lack of it.

Plenty of people believe that you are not supposed to have boundaries in relationships. This is a flawed concept because if you don't have any boundaries, you practically don't exist in the relationship. You are invisible. And the last I checked, relationships require two individuals. It takes two to tango.

Once you understand that you need to have your personal boundaries, you also begin to respect and be okay with other's boundaries too. This is when Respect comes into a relationship - one of the essential ingredients for healthy connections. Love and respect are two different things, and you cannot have one without the other.

Therapist's Interpretation: There are different kinds of boundaries - porous, non-existent, like strong solid walls or like a beautiful fence.

- Porous boundaries leave people confused as to what you are okay with and where to draw the line. This creates a chaotic relationship.
- Non-existent boundaries are a sign of co-dependent relationships, which essentially means, one partner is oxygen for the other partner. This leads to clingy, possessive and obsessive behaviour leading the other person to suffocate.
- Strong solid walls make you invisible, unreachable and cut you off from your loved ones. Usually, as a result of getting hurt by someone trusted in the past, these walls don't let you connect and have authentic relationships with anyone. You end up feeling like you cannot be yourself in the relationship and your partner never gets to know the real you.
- Boundaries like a beautiful fence are the healthiest. They tell people where you draw the line, they also communicate when it is ok for the other person to step in (with permission) and they help you create healthier relationships.

Understand your boundaries, learn to create them and remember that if you don't respect your boundaries, no one else will.

Rule No.5: *Know Your Reasons To Be In A Relationship*

Ever wondered why you want to be in a relationship?

Are you getting into a relationship because you feel lonely, or because that is what everyone else is doing? Do you want a relationship to feel secure or because the sex is good?

It is a good idea to know your reasons. A good reason to be in a relationship is that you want to share your life, and the goodness in it. Because if the reason is anything besides this, it is most likely a transaction.

There are certain laws of nature or the universe like the law of cause and effect, the law of attraction, etc., that are always operating. One of these is the Law of Reflection. If you are getting into a relationship to fulfil a need, the other person is also in it for the same reason - to fulfil a need. You give me something so I will give you something - love, time, money, attention, sex, etc.

Transactions are not love. When there is no love, that relationship is bound to run out of juice soon. When the initial high of having the need fulfilled is over, it will start to feel like a trap, there will be suffocation, feeling of being stuck and negative feelings in the relationship.

At this point, most people decide to call it quits and begin to look for "love" again. And inevitably another cycle ensues.

To escape this cycle, it is necessary to know what need you are trying to fulfil through a relationship and fulfil it for yourself. It is said that when you don't need someone, that is when you find the one who can share love with you.

Relationships are not business deals or transactions. They are meant to be about sharing. You can't share something that you don't have - remember that.

Therapist's Interpretation: Humans have a few basic needs - love, comfort, safety and connection. Comfort and safety are the primal needs. Love and connection come into the picture when you are not running for your survival.

Trauma keeps us in survival mode. If you feel you have difficulty connecting to people, have difficult relationships, have problems with being authentic and have fears of judgment or criticism that are affecting your ability to form healthy bonds, it is time to reach out to a therapist to help yourself.

Seeking relationships without healing is akin to seeking substances to suppress the discomfort that you are feeling. It becomes an addiction. Relationships then become a compulsion, they are not about choice then.

Once your traumas are healing, then it would be a good time to re-evaluate your reasons to be in a relationship and seek someone out.

In a nutshell

There are many more things - big and small - that can help you with having better relationships. But it all begins with the self. Remember, you can't share what you don't have. So focus on building your inventory of feeling good about yourself, know what you bring to the table before asking what others bring to it and continue on your personal growth and healing journey to keep your relationships healthy and happy.

About the writer

Meetu Sehgal

Meetu Sehgal is a Personal Transformation and Emotional Wellness Coach, EFT Trainer, Tarot Reader, Author, Reiki Grandmaster and Counselling Psychologist. With more than 15 years of experience in her field, she has been passionately working with individuals, helping them resolve health, wealth and relationship challenges through coaching. Meetu Sehgal is an MBA graduate from Delhi University and also holds a Masters in Psychology. Passionate about writing and spirituality, she has blended both in her work, which has helped hundreds of people around the world find peace within themselves. Her latest book, "Happy Inside Out", is a definitive guide to understanding and handling emotions and moods.

III

The Psychology of Love: Understanding Attachment in Relationships

The Psychology of Love:
Understanding Attachment in Relationships

The chairman of Larsen & Toubro (L&T), sparked an online outrage with his comments advocating a 90-hour work week and suggesting that employees should even give up Sundays. In a purported video, he addressed employees, urging them to spend less time at home and more in the office.

India's work-life balance is a topic for discussion in another article, another day. Today, we would like to address this outrage from a different angle.

"How long can you stare at your wife?" While this statement may seem light-hearted at first, it reflects a deeper societal issue. When did our relationships become so insignificant, and where did the importance of our loved ones get lost? In our relentless pursuit of professional success, have we become slaves to our jobs, prioritizing deadlines over dinner conversations and emails over emotional connections? The bonds we once cherished seem to wither under the weight of work stress and ambition, leaving our partners and loved ones yearning for the attention and presence they deserve. It begs us to reflect: is the legacy of our lives defined by our career achievements and social media following, or by the love, memories, and meaning we create with those closest to us in real time?

Human beings are inherently social creatures, and relationships play a central role in our well-being, development, and fulfilment. Relationships, whether romantic, familial, platonic, or professional, provide emotional support, help us grow, and offer a sense of purpose and belonging. Cultivating healthy relationships positively impacts both physical and mental health through scientifically proven mechanisms. It has been proven, that our relationships significantly influence our biology and overall well-being.

Effect of Healthy Relationships on Mind and Body

Here's a detailed exploration of the science behind how healthy relationships improve body chemistry, mental health, and physical health:

1. Relationships and the Oxytocin Effect

- **Science**: Oxytocin, known as the "love hormone," is released during positive social interactions, such as hugs, kind words, or physical touch. It enhances bonding, trust, and emotional connection.

- **Health Benefits**:

  - Reduces stress by lowering cortisol levels.
  - Promotes relaxation and improves sleep quality.
  - Enhances feelings of safety and emotional security.

- **Example**: Studies show that hugging or holding hands with a loved one can significantly decrease blood pressure and heart rate, reducing the risk of cardiovascular issues.

2. Reduced Stress and Cortisol Regulation

- **Science**: Healthy relationships buffer against chronic stress by providing emotional support, which prevents prolonged activation of the hypothalamic-pituitary-adrenal (HPA) axis, the body's stress response system.
- **Health Benefits**:

  - Decreased inflammation in the body.
  - Lower risk of stress-related illnesses like heart disease, diabetes, and depression.
  - Improved digestion and immunity.

- **Example**: Research from the American Psychological Association shows that people in supportive relationships have lower cortisol levels compared to those in toxic or strained relationships.

3. Improved Immune System

- **Science**: Positive relationships reduce stress hormones and increase the production of natural killer cells and white blood cells, which fight infections and maintain immune health.
- **Health Benefits**:

- ◦ Faster recovery from illness or injury.
- ◦ Lower susceptibility to colds, flu, and other infections.
- ◦ Reduced risk of autoimmune disorders.

- **Example**: A study published in *Psychosomatic Medicine* found that individuals in happy marriages healed from wounds faster than those in conflicted relationships.

4. Cardiovascular Health

- **Science**: Love, affection, and emotional support improve heart health by reducing stress, improving heart rate variability, and lowering blood pressure.
- **Health Benefits**:

  - ◦ Decreased risk of heart attacks and strokes.
  - ◦ Improved circulation and cardiovascular function.

- **Example**: A Harvard study found that people with strong social connections had a 50% greater likelihood of survival from cardiovascular events compared to those who were socially isolated.

5. Mental Health Boost: Dopamine and Serotonin

- **Science**: Healthy relationships trigger the release of dopamine (the "feel-good" neurotransmitter) and serotonin, which regulate mood, happiness, and overall mental health.
- **Health Benefits**:

  - ◦ Reduced symptoms of anxiety and depression.
  - ◦ Improved mood and emotional resilience.
  - ◦ Enhanced motivation and optimism.

- **Example**: People in loving relationships or strong friendships report higher levels of life satisfaction and emotional stability, according to research published in *The Journal of Positive Psychology*.

6. Longevity and Reduced Mortality Risk

- **Science**: Social connections activate pathways in the brain associated with longevity and reduce inflammation that contributes to ageing-related diseases.
- **Health Benefits**:

  - Increased life expectancy.
  - Delayed onset of chronic diseases.

- **Example**: The *Harvard Study of Adult Development* showed that quality relationships are a stronger predictor of longevity and happiness than wealth, IQ, or genetics.

7. Pain Management

- **Science**: Positive relationships influence the brain's pain centres. Oxytocin and endorphins released in healthy relationships act as natural painkillers.
- **Health Benefits**:

  - Reduced perception of physical pain.
  - Enhanced recovery from surgeries or chronic pain conditions.

- **Example**: Research shows that people holding hands with a loved one experience less pain during stressful situations.

8. Enhanced Sleep Quality

- **Science**: Emotional support and secure relationships help regulate the parasympathetic nervous system, which is essential for restorative sleep.
- **Health Benefits**:

  - Reduced insomnia and better REM sleep.
  - Improved cognitive function and emotional balance.

- **Example**: Couples in healthy relationships are more likely to report uninterrupted sleep compared to those in strained relationships.

9. Cognitive Health

- **Science**: Social interaction stimulates brain function, keeps neural connections active, and reduces the risk of cognitive decline.
- **Health Benefits**:

  - Improved memory and focus.
  - Reduced risk of dementia and Alzheimer's disease.

- **Example**: Studies have found that older adults with strong social ties are less likely to develop cognitive impairment.

10. Lower Risk of Mental Illness

- **Science**: Supportive relationships provide a buffer against psychological disorders by fostering a sense of belonging and purpose.
- **Health Benefits**:

  - Lower incidence of PTSD, depression, and anxiety.
  - Increased resilience to traumatic events.

- **Example**: A supportive partner can help regulate emotional responses during a crisis, reducing the long-term mental health impact.

In Short, you may not be able to stare at your wife/Husband all the time. But you cannot spend your entire day working at the office either. You need a job/business/profession to pay your bills and afford your lifestyle. But you need your relationships to have a life and to share the joy of enjoying all that money. Don't you think so? Then, you probably fall into an **insecure attachment style**.

Attachment Styles

Mary Ainsworth through her "Strange Situation" experiment introduced the concept of attachment styles, which was developed upon the work of British psychologist John Bowlby. Attachment styles are psychological patterns that describe how individuals form emotional bonds with others. These patterns are shaped by early interactions with primary caregivers and continue to influence our relationships throughout life.

There are two primary attachment styles:

1. **Secure Attachment**: A **secure attachment style** is a way of relating to others in relationships characterized by trust, emotional balance, and healthy communication. It typically develops in childhood when caregivers are consistently responsive, supportive, and nurturing.
2. **Insecure Attachment Style:** An insecure attachment style is a way of relating to others in relationships marked by fear, uncertainty, or instability. It typically develops in childhood due to inconsistent, neglectful, or overly controlling caregiving. There are three kinds of insecure attachment styles:

    a. **Anxious Attachment**: Marked by fear of abandonment, a need for constant reassurance, and emotional dependency, craving closeness but often feeling insecure.
    b. **Avoidant Attachment**: Defined by discomfort with intimacy, emotional distancing, and a tendency to prioritize independence, avoiding vulnerability.
    c. **Disorganized Attachment**: A mix of anxious and avoidant behaviours, often stemming from trauma or inconsistent caregiving.

Healing attachment styles is a transformative process that not only improves your relationships but also enhances your emotional well-being. It requires self-awareness, inner work, and consistent effort.

The goal of healing is to move toward a **secure attachment style** where emotional intimacy and autonomy are balanced. In this article, you will find a detailed guide with **solutions for healing attachment styles** and actionable steps to cultivate healthier relationships.

The Role of Attachment Styles in Relationships

Attachment styles play a pivotal role in shaping how individuals:

1. **Form Emotional Bonds**: Securely attached individuals are more likely to build strong, healthy relationships.
2. **Communicate**: Anxious individuals may over-communicate, while avoidant individuals may under-communicate.
3. **Handle Conflict**: Secure attachment fosters constructive conflict resolution, while insecure styles may lead to escalation or avoidance.
4. **Express Vulnerability**: Anxious and secure styles lean into vulnerability, while avoidant and disorganized styles resist it.
5. **Set Boundaries**: Securely attached people are better at setting and respecting boundaries.
6. **Trust**: Anxious and disorganized styles often struggle with trust.
7. **Navigate Dependency**: Secure individuals balance independence and interdependence, unlike insecure styles.
8. **Resolve Trauma**: Attachment styles influence how partners support each other in healing.
9. **Build Intimacy**: Secure attachment facilitates emotional and physical intimacy.
10. **Commit**: Avoidant individuals may fear commitment, while anxious individuals might rush it.

Stages of a Relationship and Attachment Styles

Relationships often go through distinct stages as they develop and deepen over time. These stages reflect the natural progression of emotional connection, intimacy, and growth. Understanding these stages can help individuals navigate the complexities of relationships more effectively and address challenges with greater awareness.

1. Initial Attraction

Overview: This is the beginning phase, often called the "honeymoon stage." It is characterised by physical attraction, excitement, and curiosity about the other person.
Key Features:

1. Intense chemistry and infatuation.
2. Idealization of the other person.
3. Desire to spend a lot of time together.
4. Exploration of shared interests and values.
5. A focus on physical appearance and charm.
6. Conversations often center around surface-level topics.
7. Minimal conflict due to the novelty of the relationship.
8. Dopamine spikes from romantic interactions, creating euphoria.
9. Overlooking flaws due to the "rose-coloured glasses" effect.
10. High energy and optimism about the potential future.

Challenges:

- Overlooking red flags.
- Confusing attraction with compatibility.
- Rushing into commitments prematurely.

Attachment Styles: Secure individuals feel confident in approaching others, while avoidant people may hesitate, and anxious individuals might overanalyze every interaction.

2. Building Connection

Overview: As the initial excitement stabilizes, both partners begin to build emotional intimacy and deepen their understanding of each other.
Key Features:

1. Developing trust through shared experiences.
2. Honest conversations about beliefs, goals, and fears.
3. Beginning to show vulnerability.

4. Discovering compatibility in communication styles.
5. Increased focus on emotional and intellectual connection.
6. Balancing individuality with togetherness.
7. Recognizing and appreciating each other's quirks.
8. Building routines and shared activities.
9. Testing compatibility in values and life goals.
10. Beginning to handle minor conflicts or misunderstandings.

Challenges:

- Fear of vulnerability or rejection.
- Misalignment of long-term goals.
- Struggles with balancing independence and dependence.

Attachment Styles: Anxious partners may cling, avoidants might withdraw, and secure individuals foster open communication.

3. Deepening Intimacy

Overview: This stage involves a deeper emotional, physical, and spiritual connection. Both partners feel secure and comfortable being their authentic selves.

Key Features:

1. Open discussions about fears, dreams, and insecurities.
2. Increased physical and emotional intimacy.
3. Establishing a sense of partnership and shared identity.
4. Feeling safe and accepted for who you are.
5. Shared decision-making and goal-setting.
6. Stronger emotional resilience as a couple.
7. Exploring deeper compatibility, including spiritual or philosophical alignment.
8. Greater tolerance for each other's flaws.
9. Building a long-term vision for the relationship.
10. Handling conflict with maturity and empathy.

Challenges:

- Navigating disagreements without compromising individuality.
- Addressing past traumas that surface in deeper intimacy.
- Managing external pressures such as family or societal expectations.

Attachment Styles: Avoidants may struggle to open up, while anxious partners may seek constant reassurance. Secures encourage mutual vulnerability.

4. Commitment

Overview: This stage solidifies the relationship. Partners decide to invest in each other for the long term, whether through marriage, partnership, or a mutual agreement.

Key Features:

1. Formalizing the relationship (e.g., engagement, moving in together).
2. Shared vision for the future (e.g., family planning, financial goals).
3. Building a sense of security and loyalty.
4. Mutual support during life challenges.
5. Creating shared traditions and routines.
6. Celebrating milestones as a couple.
7. Strong communication and conflict-resolution skills.
8. Demonstrating unwavering trust and dependability.
9. Balancing personal growth with the growth of the relationship.
10. Deepening interdependence while maintaining individuality.

Challenges:

- Complacency or taking each other for granted.
- Balancing individual aspirations with relationship goals.
- Handling external stresses such as finances or family dynamics.

Attachment Styles: Avoidants might feel trapped, anxious partners may fear abandonment and secure focus on shared goals.

5. Maintenance

Overview: In this phase, couples work to keep the relationship healthy, exciting, and fulfilling over time. This stage often involves long-term effort and adaptability.

Key Features:

1. Continuous communication and checking in with each other.
2. Revisiting and revising shared goals.
3. Keeping romance alive through intentional efforts.
4. Navigating life changes together (e.g., career shifts, parenting, ageing).
5. Prioritizing quality time despite busy schedules.
6. Supporting each other's personal growth.
7. Balancing shared responsibilities (e.g., finances, household tasks).
8. Conflict management through constructive conversations.
9. Maintaining mutual respect and appreciation.
10. Celebrating achievements and milestones.

Challenges:

- Risk of falling into monotonous routines.
- Struggles with adapting to major life changes.
- Potential for emotional drift if effort is not maintained.

Attachment Styles: Anxious individuals may micromanage the relationship, and avoidants might prioritize independence and secure focus on growth and adaptability.

6. Conflict Resolution and Growth

Overview: Conflicts are inevitable, but how a couple navigates them determines the strength and longevity of the relationship.

Key Features:

1. Identifying and addressing recurring issues.
2. Practicing empathy and active listening.
3. Learning to compromise without resentment.
4. Building emotional resilience as a team.
5. Turning challenges into opportunities for growth.
6. Acknowledging and apologizing for mistakes.

7. Seeking external support when needed (e.g., therapy).
8. Establishing healthy boundaries.
9. Forgiving and letting go of past grievances.
10. Strengthening the relationship through adversity.

Challenges:

- Miscommunication or defensiveness.
- Difficulty in letting go of resentment or grudges.
- Balancing personal triggers with relationship dynamics.

Attachment Styles: Secures resolve issues collaboratively, anxious individuals may overreact, and avoidants might shut down.

7. Renewal or Dissolution

Overview: Relationships evolve, and this stage involves either renewing the bond with greater depth or deciding to part ways.
Key Features:

1. Reflecting on the relationship's journey and current state.
2. Deepening emotional and physical intimacy.
3. Reaffirming commitments and shared goals.
4. Rebuilding trust if it has been shaken.
5. Making significant life decisions together.
6. Reassessing compatibility and alignment of values.
7. Investing in personal growth for mutual benefit.
8. Recognizing when the relationship no longer serves both partners.
9. Ending the relationship with maturity and respect if necessary.
10. Finding closure and moving forward, individually or together.

Challenges:

- Fear of change or loss.
- Struggles with accepting differences or incompatibilities.
- Emotional distress if the relationship ends.

Attachment Styles: Secure individuals handle breakups maturely, while anxious and avoidant partners may exhibit unhealthy coping mechanisms.

Attachment Styles and Millennials/Gen Z

Millennials and Gen Z often exhibit unique relational patterns influenced by societal, technological, and cultural shifts. Here's how attachment styles are relevant to these generations:

1. **Technology Dependence**: Growing up with social media and smartphones has altered how these generations form and maintain attachments.
2. **Rise of Individualism**: There's an emphasis on self-reliance, which can exacerbate avoidant tendencies.
3. **Delayed Life Milestones**: Economic challenges and shifting priorities mean relationships often take a backseat.
4. **Swipe Culture**: Dating apps promote casual connections, which may amplify insecure attachment behaviours.
5. **Mental Health Awareness**: Greater awareness of mental health has led to more conversations about attachment patterns.
6. **Changing Family Dynamics**: Higher divorce rates and non-traditional family structures have influenced attachment development.
7. **Hyper-Connectivity**: Instant communication can lead to both closeness and over-dependence.
8. **Comparison Culture**: Social media fosters unrealistic relationship expectations.
9. **Fear of Vulnerability**: Avoidant behaviours are often normalized as "playing it cool."
10. **Therapy Normalization**: Many Millennials and Gen Z are actively addressing attachment wounds through therapy.

Modern Dating Scenarios and Attachment Styles

1. **Swipe Culture & Dating App Fatigue**: Avoidants thrive in low-commitment environments and disengage entirely while anxious individuals may struggle with rejection and may feel overwhelmed.

2. **Ghosting**: Ghosting happens when someone suddenly cuts off all communication without explanation, leaving the other person confused and hurt. Disorganized and avoidant styles often ghost; anxious individuals are deeply affected by it.

3. **Hookup Culture**: Avoidants prefer casual relationships; anxious individuals often seek emotional validation through hookups.

4. **Texting Etiquette**: Anxious partners may become addicted to constant communication or overthink delayed replies, while avoidants may avoid frequent texting. Texts and posts are easily misinterpreted leading to miscommunication.

5. **Social Media Influence**: Social media has increasingly been linked to fostering narcissistic tendencies in individuals, largely due to its design and cultural impact. Comparison and insecurity can exacerbate attachment anxieties. It has been observed that Avoidants use social media for emotional distancing as a barrier to intimacy. Seeing a partner's interactions on social media can heighten insecurities.

How social media contributes to the rise of narcissism:

1. Hyper-Focus on Self-Presentation

Social media platforms encourage users to carefully curate and present an idealized version of themselves. This creates an environment where people invest significant time and energy into creating the "perfect" image, boosting their sense of self-importance. Validation becomes tied to external metrics such as likes, followers, and comments, fueling self-centred behaviour.

2. Instant Gratification and Validation

Social media provides **immediate feedback** through likes, shares, and comments, which can act as dopamine triggers. Anxious individuals rely heavily on likes and comments for self-esteem. This instant gratification encourages people to post more frequently to seek continued validation. Over time, reliance on external validation can lead to self-centeredness and reduced concern for others' feelings or perspectives.

3. Comparison Culture

Social media fosters unrealistic relationship standards. Constant exposure to others' highlight reels fosters unhealthy comparisons, leading individuals to overcompensate by crafting exaggerated or false portrayals of their own lives. The need to outshine others can reinforce egotistical tendencies and a focus on personal success over meaningful connections.

4. Metrics of Popularity

Social media metrics, like follower counts and engagement rates, create a **quantifiable measure of social value**, encouraging individuals to chase numbers instead of genuine relationships. This gamification of social worth reinforces narcissistic tendencies by tying self-esteem to digital approval.

5. Celebrity Culture and Influencer Idealization

The rise of influencers and micro-celebrities on platforms like Instagram and TikTok glamorizes narcissistic traits such as self-promotion and the pursuit of fame. People aspire to mimic these behaviours, focusing on personal branding and attention-seeking over authenticity.

6. Echo Chambers

Algorithms prioritize content that receives the most engagement, often rewarding extreme, self-promotional, or sensationalized behaviour. This creates echo chambers where narcissistic tendencies are validated and amplified by others with similar mindsets.

7. Oversharing and Boundary Issues

Social media blurs the lines between private and public life, leading people to overshare personal details to garner attention or sympathy. Constant online presence reduces mystery and novelty. This lack of boundaries can reinforce the belief that everyone else's lives are more important or deserving of attention than your own.

8. Reduced Empathy

Excessive use of social media can diminish face-to-face interactions, leading to a decline in empathy and emotional intelligence. Narcissistic individuals may struggle to understand or care about others' emotions due to the impersonal nature of digital communication.

9. FOMO and Envy

Social media perpetuates the **fear of missing out (FOMO)** and envy by showcasing others' seemingly perfect lives. It amplifies anxiety about being left out or unloved. This can lead individuals to become hyper-focused on projecting an image of success and superiority. **Online Curated Perfection** affects both avoidant and anxious individuals who may struggle with authenticity.

10. Superficial Relationships

Many social media connections lack depth, encouraging surface-level interactions. This can lead to an inflated sense of self-worth while diminishing the importance of genuine, empathetic connections.

1. **Long-Distance Relationships**: Secure individuals adapt well, while insecure styles struggle with trust and communicating their needs in the relationship.
2. **Open Relationships**: Avoidants may find this appealing as there is a lack of commitment and accountability, while anxious individuals may struggle with jealousy and insecurity.
3. **Bread-Crumbing**: Breadcrumbing occurs when someone gives sporadic, non-committal attention to keep another person interested without the intention of pursuing a meaningful relationship. Avoidants often engage in this behaviour, leaving anxious individuals confused.
4. **Fear of Labels**: Avoidants resist defining relationships, causing distress for anxious partners.

Solutions to Counteract Social Media-Induced Narcissism

1. **Digital Detox:** Regularly taking breaks from social media can reduce reliance on external validation.
2. **Focus on Authenticity:** Emphasize genuine connections and honest self-expression over curated perfection.
3. **Mindfulness Practices:** Reflect on your intentions for using social media and stay mindful of its effects on your mental health.
4. **Limit Social Media Metrics:** Avoid fixating on likes and follower counts; prioritize meaningful engagement instead.
5. **Promote Empathy:** Engage in activities that encourage understanding and care for others, like volunteering or active listening.
6. **Encourage Media Literacy:** Educate yourself on the impact of algorithms and the curated nature of content.
7. **Cultivate Offline Relationships:** Spend more time nurturing real-life relationships that foster emotional depth.
8. **Therapy:** Seek professional guidance to address deeper insecurities or patterns of narcissistic behaviour.
9. **Diversify Content Consumption:** Follow creators and accounts that inspire empathy, learning, or self-improvement rather than competition.

10. **Set Boundaries**: Limit screen time and avoid social media use in emotionally vulnerable moments.

By being mindful of how social media shapes behaviour, individuals can reduce narcissistic tendencies and focus on fostering genuine, empathetic relationships both online and offline.

Solutions for Healing Attachment Styles and Relationships

1. Develop Self-Awareness

Understanding your attachment style is the first step to healing.
Action Steps:

- **Identify Your Attachment Style**: Take quizzes or work with a therapist to understand your patterns.
- **Journal Your Triggers**: Write down situations that make you feel insecure, distant, or overly dependent.
- **Reflect on Past Relationships**: Identify recurring themes, such as fear of abandonment or avoiding emotional intimacy.
- **Educate Yourself**: Read books and resources on attachment theory (*Attached* by Amir Levine is a great start, I Got Love By Ashi Sharma- Coming Soon)

2. Practice Emotional Regulation

Healing attachment often involves managing intense emotions, such as fear, anger, or anxiety, in a healthy way.
Action Steps:

1. **Breathing Techniques**: Use deep breathing or box breathing to calm your nervous system.
2. **Grounding Exercises**: Techniques like mindfulness or focusing on your senses can help you stay present.
3. **Label Your Emotions**: Naming your feelings can help you process them effectively.

3. Improve Communication Skills

Healthy relationships require clear and open communication, regardless of your attachment style.

Action Steps:

- Practice Assertiveness: Learn to express your needs and feelings calmly and respectfully.
- Active Listening: Pay attention to your partner's words without interrupting or becoming defensive.
- Use "I" Statements: Say, "I feel hurt when..." instead of blaming, e.g., "You always..."

4. Work Through Disorganized Attachment

Disorganized attachment often involves unresolved trauma, requiring deeper healing.

Action Steps:

- Therapy for Trauma: Work with a therapist specializing in trauma-focused modalities like EMDR or somatic therapy.
- Inner Child Work: Connect with your younger self to address fears and insecurities.
- Safe Relationships: Seek partners or friendships that provide consistent, supportive interactions.

5. Set and Respect Boundaries

Boundaries are essential for all attachment styles to ensure mutual respect and safety.

Action Steps:

- Clarify Your Boundaries: Know your limits regarding time, energy, and emotional involvement.
- Communicate Clearly: Express boundaries directly but kindly, e.g., "I need space to process my feelings."
- Respect Others' Boundaries: Avoid taking others' boundaries personally.

16. Seek Professional Help

Therapy can accelerate the healing process by addressing deep-seated issues and providing guidance.

Action Steps:

- Choose the Right Therapist: Look for someone trained in attachment theory, relationships or trauma recovery.
- Use Therapeutic Tools: Explore Cognitive Behavioral Therapy (CBT), Emotional Freedom Techniques (EFT), or somatic practices.
- Be Patient with Yourself: Healing attachment wounds takes time and consistent effort.

Healing attachment styles is a journey, not a destination. By committing to consistent self-growth, fostering emotional intelligence, and practicing self-compassion, you can build healthier relationships and create a more fulfilling emotional life to combat the lack of depth in modern-day connections.

About the Writer

Ashi Sharma

Ashi Sharma is a multi-faceted professional and an inspiring force in the realms of personal development and holistic healing. As an author, expressive arts therapy practitioner, EFT practitioner, tarot healer, and podcaster at Breaking Mythos, she brings a unique blend of insights to her work as a Reiki master, lifestyle and business coach and consultant. She has been honoured in the BW Wellbeing World 30 Under 30 Awards for the year 2022 and 2023. Her latest work is part of a beautiful coffee table book, 'Mythology' enriched with hand-painted illustrations that bring ancient stories and legends to life. In this book, she talks about the spiritual journeys of Shukracharya and Odin.

IV

You Wanted an Alpha, But Married an Empath: Here's Why Marrying an Empath Might Be the Better Choice

You Wanted an Alpha, But Married an Empath:
Here's Why Marrying an Empath Might Be the Better Choice

We don't always get what we want. Some say 'It's the fault in our stars." while others like to blame society, their parents, their upbringing, poverty... and the list goes on. But what is the truth behind what we get in life? Is it really all these factors, or is there more to it? Well, I, for one, always thought we can't change anything because, well, destiny.

I was brought up in a house where every second sentence would be, "I guess he was destined to have that", or "What's destined to happen will happen". And so, I believed that too.

For a very long time.

Until I learnt otherwise.

Though I'm still a believer, there are times when I question certain things, behaviours and beliefs.

A Real Story Searching for Fantasy

A guy at work seemed nice at first. He was always taking charge at work in terms of managing things for the team. He fitted well with my definitions of being an alpha, and I thought to myself my fantasies were finally coming true. It was very strange to me and something that had never happened before, but when I casually hinted at grabbing a coffee with him sometime, he instantly agreed. Without even giving it a thought. As if I had just said out loud what he wished secretly and maybe even planned a better way to ask me out. Who knows.

So here we were from the coffee on that rainy August evening to getting married 3 years later. Both our parents were in total agreement (another strange thing). Not that I'm always looking for complications, but it just felt too easy. You know what I mean?

Turns out, maybe, I was looking for problems.

A few months after we got married, I didn't feel the same way about him. I felt like he wasn't the alpha I thought him to be. He would understand things that were going on in my mind without me saying it. He would mostly make dinner, knowing my work shift was different than his, and I always got late. We had different jobs later on, so he would always make time to listen to how my day was.

Something didn't feel right. Despite him being a very nice person overall, I just didn't feel the spark in the bedroom with him. I always wanted an alpha to take charge both in real life and in the bedroom, too. It just didn't make sense to me later on. While on one hand, he was the nicest husband on the planet, he wasn't an alpha and that, to me, was a problem. So, I tried communicating my needs to him. I thought it would solve things, and it did to an extent. He understood the points I was trying to make and worked on each of them as if he was assigned a task-sincerity and dedication.

He could see my frustration piling up over the months, and though he did ask a few times, I wasn't in the mind space to talk about it. A year into our marriage, I still wasn't sure what was wrong. He did everything I asked. He even went out of his way to throw in a few surprises every now and then, just as I had explained the concept of alpha to him. He knew I wasn't up for monotony, and deep down, I still felt the void. I didn't know what was wrong, but no matter what he tried, I wasn't feeling the connection.

Another few months passed, and I met with a friend of mine one day. When she started to describe her unhappy marriage, I listened closely to perhaps understand something about my own. After several hours of her non-stop rant and a few pieces of advice I gave her, I realised hers couldn't be fixed because she married the wrong person. He didn't treat her with respect, didn't consider her opinion for anything, communicated poorly about most of the things, and missed a lot of events that were important to her.

That evening, when I went home, I saw my empath-turned-alpha husband dressed up in a suit and asking me questions about where I was and why I got so late for dinner. (Something I asked him to do as it meant showing concern for me) I went closer to hug him. I realised what I had been looking for all this time was perhaps not good for me. If I was indeed the kind of marriage my friend described she was in, or for that matter any other marriage, I wouldn't be happy. This guy, right here, in front of me, making so much of an effort to understand me better and to support me in every way possible, has always been a blessing.

Understanding the Problem

So, what exactly was my problem? Well, it turns out that a normal relationship seems boring, and that drama was something that would add that excitement and adrenaline rush into my life. What's better to do just that than arguments and fights with your partner? Only to make up later on.

But this was becoming exhausting, and the conversation with my friend made me see this non-existent problem that I was creating much more clearly. It made me realise that maybe all I needed was to change my perspective about this 'alpha' personality. After all, my husband did take charge of the situation. He did show up in every way possible. He did provide space for me. (This exact moment when I wanted to go thank my mother-in-law for the amazing son she raised for another time!)

Everything an alpha does in movies, series etc, he did all that. His face might be that of a sweet guy but deep down, he was the alpha I was looking for. It was all about perspective. In all fairness, if I had communicated this earlier, it wouldn't have taken so long for me to figure out what was going on but my husband was still patient all through this process.

To answer the question of 'you wanted an alpha but married an empath: what to do?' I'd say thank the God above for this blessing. Maybe this empath is your alpha, or maybe they aren't. Going on a wild goose chase for something that isn't there and letting go of something beautiful that's right in front of you is definitely a mistake you don't want to make!

&

I'm Samara. Maybe even you are. Perhaps we all have been in her place one day or another. Understanding relationships may take a while and tremendous effort sometimes but appreciating what's right in front of you and making the most of it, can take you on a happy journey for sure. My gut told me something wasn't right and I chased that feeling only to realise what was really going on here. One has to be really honest about that and that, again, is an effort that you need for relationships to work.

About the Writer

Arushi Sharma

Arushi is a PhD candidate in Law at Trinity College Dublin and her research work revolves around Data Protection in the financial sector. A full-time law student and a part-time energy worker, she is passionate about teaching and learning. With more than 7 years of experience in healing, she firmly believes in the transformative power of self-reflection and the guidance that each healing offers. Her offerings as a healer and coach help individuals navigate challenges and confidently embrace opportunities.

V

Breadcrumbs, Ghosts, and Nanoships: Understanding the Complex World of Modern Relationships

Breadcrumbs, Ghosts, and Nanoships:
Understanding the Complex World of Modern Relationships

Relationships are never simple. They demand energy, emotional investment, and a willingness to grow. In today's world, where the internet provides endless advice and societal norms shape our views, distinguishing between a red flag and a green one can be overwhelming. *The rise of hook-up culture, along with the evolving views on relationships among Gen Z and Gen Alpha, has added new layers of complexity to how people connect and define their relationships.*

But amidst all this noise, the pursuit of meaningful connections remains universal. So how do you navigate this intricate web of emotions, expectations, and realities?

New Relationship Dynamics

- **Situationship**: A grey area between casual dating and a committed relationship. It lacks clear labels, often leaving both partners uncertain about where they stand.
- **Breadcrumbing**: When someone leads you on by giving intermittent attention, keeping you interested without any intention of committing.
- **Ghosting**: The act of abruptly cutting off all communication without explanation. It's a common but emotionally jarring phenomenon in today's dating culture.
- **Zombieing**: When someone who previously ghosted you reappears unexpectedly, trying to reestablish contact as if nothing happened.
- **Nanoship**: A very recent term that refers to ultra-short-lived connections—relationships that dissolve almost as quickly as they begin.

These dynamics often blur the lines of traditional dating, introducing confusion and sometimes emotional distress. While they highlight the evolving nature of relationships, they also underscore the importance of clear communication and emotional boundaries.

The Quest for the Perfect Match

Let's start with a hard truth: perfection doesn't exist. You're not looking for someone flawless; instead, you're seeking someone whose imperfections you can embrace. Relationships are like solving a tricky math problem, often involving trial and error. You may get it wrong initially, but each experience teaches you something valuable, guiding you closer to the right connection.

While nothing in life is truly permanent, some relationships can come close. The key lies in making conscious choices and investing in partnerships that feel right for you—ones where growth and mutual respect thrive.

The Silent Influence of Society and Social Media

It's easy to believe you've found "the one" when society and social media constantly bombard you with ideals of love and relationships. However, these influences often distort reality, leading you to make choices based on external pressures rather than your genuine feelings.

Take, for example, the phenomenon of the "College Wife/Husband." In such relationships, one partner may seem committed, but the bond is often rooted in convenience rather than authenticity. As the college phase ends, so does the relationship, leaving one person hurt and emotionally drained.

These experiences serve as reminders to approach relationships with clarity and self-awareness, ensuring your choices reflect your true desires rather than societal expectations.

The Core of Healthy Relationships

Healthy relationships aren't about sacrifice or losing yourself. They thrive on mutual effort, where both individuals contribute equally and prioritize each other's well-being while fostering their own growth.

Love is not about completing another person; it's about growing alongside them. This growth involves healing past wounds, accepting harsh realities, and becoming your best self—not just for your partner but for your own happiness.

Healing is crucial. It's about confronting your traumas and learning from them, enabling you to approach relationships with a fresh perspective and an open heart.

Love Is a Journey, Not a Destination

One of the most common mistakes people make in relationships is taking their partner for granted once a sense of security is established.

Relationships require constant nurturing. Without effort and understanding, even the strongest bonds can deteriorate, leading to jealousy, resentment, or unresolved conflicts.

To keep love alive, view it as an evolving journey rather than a destination. This mindset encourages continuous growth and strengthens the bond between you and your partner.

Building a Deeper Connection

True intimacy comes from understanding your partner on a deeper level. Asking meaningful questions can help foster this connection and ensure compatibility. Here are some questions to consider:

- **Have you ever felt unheard or overburdened by your emotions?**
  This question can reveal their mental state and emotional needs, opening the door for meaningful support.
- **What are your insecurities and fears?**
  Encouraging your partner to share their vulnerabilities builds trust and fosters a safe space for honest communication.
- **Do you feel this relationship needs more—like better communication or more quality time?**
  Knowing their expectations allows you to address gaps and strengthen your connection.
- **Have you experienced something in the past that still affects you?**
  Understanding their triggers helps you navigate sensitive areas with empathy and care.
- **What is your love language? How do you prefer to give and receive love?**
  Learning this ensures both partners feel valued and prevents misunderstandings.

These conversations may touch on sensitive areas, so approach them with patience, compassion, and an open mind.

The Reality of Love and Effort

Life and relationships are not always fair. People can disappoint you, and love can feel elusive. However, when you find the right person, they have the power to turn life's challenges into moments of joy.

Reaching this level of deep connection isn't easy. It requires courage, resilience, and a willingness to work through obstacles together. But the rewards—a love that feels fulfilling and uplifting—are worth every effort.

Express your love openly and honestly, but always guard your emotional and physical boundaries. Remember, your strength lies within you, not in someone else's approval or presence.

Final Thoughts: A Love Worth Fighting For

Relationships are a beautiful blend of effort, growth, and shared experiences. They're not about finding someone to complete you but rather about creating a partnership that enhances both your lives.

Stay true to yourself. Embrace your journey with strength and self-awareness, and when you find the right person, nurture that connection with care and intention. Together, you can create a love story that not only stands the test of time but also brings out the best in both of you.

Because at the end of the day, love isn't just about finding the perfect partner—it's about building a relationship that's perfectly yours.

About the Writer

Chahat Singh

Deeply drawn to spirituality, Chahat is an aspiring content writer with a passion for crafting meaningful narratives. With a bachelor's degree in History and English, she is currently pursuing her masters in English. She finds inspiration in exploring the realms of inner peace and self-discovery, blending pursuits with a reflective outlook on life.

• 52 •

VI
The Heart Chakra: A Path to Unconditional Love and Meaningful Relationships

The Heart Chakra:
A Path to Unconditional Love and
Meaningful Relationships

Whenever we talk about heart, it's dil ki awaz, dil ke rishte, dil ki baaten, dil se....Sometimes we say I think from my heart; I follow my heart. All the art forms, whether it's dance, painting, or music, are expressions of our hearts, emotions, and feelings, and everyone can easily relate to this. In the chakra system, Heart Chakra relates to emotions and feelings.

Understanding the Heart Chakra: Anahata and Its Meaning

Chakra refers to the energy centres found throughout the body and each chakra is associated with major organs or nerves of the body. The heart chakra, also called the **Anahata chakra**, is located at the centre of the chest, near the heart. The major qualities of the heart chakra are unconditional love, compassion, and balance.

When our heart chakra is not in balance, our relationship with self and others is also not balanced.

Anahata is a Sanskrit word that means unstruck, unhurt or unbeaten. According to the Vedic texts, Anahata is symbolized by the image of Anahata Nada (an unstruck sound) which is pure and created within. It's a sound of the universe that only the heart can create. If you open your heart and focus on the silence within, you may be able to connect to the Anahata Nad vibration, which will connect you to everything around you.

Anahata chakra is located near the heart, in the centre of the chest, which is where every aspect of ourselves exists. The heart connects us to ourselves, the world around us, and the spiritual world. We close our eyes to pray and reach the divine through our hearts; we connect to our spiritual side through our hearts; and we love, hate, and feel different emotions through the heart. It is the centre of our being.

The Symbolism of the Heart Chakra: Colors and Divine Qualities

The heart chakra is symbolized as a green lotus with twelve petals. This symbol represents its special role in connecting the upper and lower chakras. Each petal represents one of the heart's 12 divine qualities:

1. Kindness,
2. Empathy,

3. Love,
4. Compassion,
5. Harmony,
6. Forgiveness,
7. Peace,
8. Understanding,
9. Clarity,
10. Bliss,
11. Purity and
12. Unity.

At the centre of the lotus, there is a shatkona, a six-pointed star that consists of two opposite triangles, which represent the integration of the upper and lower chakras. The star represents feminine and masculine unity.

Green and pink are the colours of the heart chakra.

Green symbolizes love, transformation, life, earth, nature, growth, and harmony. It nurtures our souls and soothes our minds. Many positive feelings are associated with green, like empathy, openness, prosperity, development, and abundance. Green is the fourth colour of the rainbow, and the heart chakra is the fourth chakra. We feel hopeful, optimistic and harmonious when we see green, and this is also connected with good health.

The heart chakra represents positive and beautiful feelings like joy and compassion. Our deepest feelings lie here, our truths that can never be described in words.

The Role of the Heart Chakra in Creating Healthy Relationships

This chakra represents love, and not only any type but unconditional love. Through love, the Anahata heals us and makes us whole. Love is the greatest healing force.

When you see and feel love in everything around you, you start to see the world differently and become kinder and more compassionate towards people in your life and yourself. When your heart chakra is open, you develop deep and meaningful relationships with others and focus on respect and empathy.

Then we feel one with the world because there is a sense of belongingness to the people, animals, trees,…An open and developed heart chakra helps us to see how we are all connected, leading us to show love to everyone we meet. This helps in developing romantic relationships and creating long-lasting friendships. We will be thoughtful towards other people's feelings and respectful of their boundaries and thoughts. The heart chakra gives you wisdom and makes you more emotionally mature and empathetic towards other's pain and suffering.

The Healing Power of the Heart Chakra: Love and Forgiveness

You become a warm person that people feel safe around. As love heals, it becomes easy to forgive and forget. It gives you the power to let go of the past and move on from the pain others have caused you. You understand that better things are coming your way, so why live in the past? Forgiveness is a choice, and you can either live with the bitterness and pain of the past or choose love and open your heart to it.

Remember how you reacted to the world around you when you were a child?

We allowed ourselves to feel and express all our emotions, whether hope, love, compassion, or even fear. We were never ashamed of our feelings. As we grow up, we become more reserved and vulnerable with our emotions.

The heart chakra helps you feel, accept, and express your different emotions with no shame, just like children. It also enables you to let go of all your childhood issues to move on from them and become better adults.

The Anahata chakra is responsible for our emotional responses and everything we feel deep inside, like our ideas, thoughts, and inspiration. It also enables you to heal, be grateful, and show generosity to the people in your life. You become someone who can create healthy relationships.

The heart chakra is a bridge between the lower and the upper chakras. When the heart is balanced, it will bring harmony and connect with the divine as deep inside our hearts lies unconditional self-acceptance.

Our life force energy is usually stagnant, but by practicing meditation, pranayam, reiki, or any techniques to unblock our chakras, it begins flowing through the Anahata. We experience various emotions like joy, self-love, and motivation, and we begin to understand the purpose of life. We let go of our superficial egos and become humble and understand that we are all connected.

The Heart Chakra's Influence on Physical Health and Well-being

The heart chakra isn't only responsible for our emotions and soul; it also has a huge impact on our physical health. It maintains the health of our immune system, blood plasma, and respiratory system. Additionally, it is connected to our vital organs and body parts, like the heart, upper back, lungs, thorax, shoulders, rib cage, and the skin and hands, due to the heart's connection to our sense of touch.

A balanced heart chakra provides you with a sense of purity and intuition. Your spiritual energy increases. Your physical health improves, your heart becomes stronger, your thyroid gland's health improves, and you notice an increase in your upper body strength. You don't seek revenge or even wish them ill if someone hurts you. This sets you free, as you are no longer driven by anger, negativity, and hatred.

An open heart chakra gives you the courage to be open and vulnerable with those close to you. You are no longer afraid of intimacy and letting go of someone. It becomes easy to trust others. You become confident and strong enough to be your most authentic self and live your own truth.

Techniques to Open and Heal the Heart Chakra

The Beatles said, "All we need is love."
Open your heart chakra and let love, joy and compassion surround you.
There are many techniques to open the heart chakra, like meditating on the heart chakra, self-analysis, wearing and using colours that represent the heart chakra, spending time with nature, and using Affirmations.
Some of the Affirmations are

1. I am open to receive and accept love.
2. I let go of past hurt and resentment.
3. I attract loving and supportive relationships.
4. I am compassionate towards myself and others.

The Bija mantra of Anahata chakra is **"YAM."** Chanting this mantra also helps balance and open the heart chakra.

The mudras to **balance and heal** the heart chakra are **Hridayaandlotus mudra.**

Crystals related to heart chakra are Rose Quartz, Malachite, Rhodonite, Jade, etc.

The essential oils related to heart chakra are Cardamom, Bergamot, Rose, and Lavender.

Using the Violet Flame for Relationship Transformation

Here is an additional secret information to open, heal, and balance the heart chakra, which is not known to many. This technique is known as Violet Flame healing. Just as we have the seven major chakras, similarly there are seven rays. Each colour of the rainbow carries distinct qualities of the Divine. Each Ray has a specific colour, frequency and quality of God's consciousness.

The violet flame is the essence of one of the seventh rays and it bears the qualities of mercy, forgiveness, and transmutation. Each Ray has a different Chohan, also known as its keeper.

St.Germain is the Ascended Master of the Seventh Ray, guardian of the violet flame.

Earlier we talked about the heart chakra's green lotus with twelve petals. Within this, there is one more secret chamber of the heart chakra where resides the Threefold Flame.

The Threefold Flame of Life is sealed in the eight-petalled chakra called the hidden, or secret chamber of the heart. This is the Violet Flame, which resides in the heart chakra in the form of a seed.

The Threefold Flame is the divine spark that makes your heart a replica of the heart of God. The Threefold Flame has three plumes that embody three primary attributes of God.

- The blue plume embodies God's power,
- The yellow gold in the centre embodies God's wisdom, and
- The pink plume embodies God's love.

The Violet Flame is one of the most powerful spiritual gifts ever given to people on earth. It's a combination of blue flame, which is divine power, yellow gold flame—divine wisdom, and pink flame—divine love. The violet flame has unlimited power to affect our lives because it is a high-frequency light that spans physical and spiritual realms. It is the vibrant spiritual light and fire that transmutes energy from the current state into a higher one. This flame is the secret, spiritual fire of alchemy with its ability to produce change. This is the highest frequency of transformational divine light.

Flames, heat, and fire have been used throughout the evolution of mankind for clearing, transformation, and in ceremonies and magic. These are also attributes of the violet flame.

For example, jyot, candle, and hawan.

The violet flame works through the power of thought, intent, and will for the highest good.

Working with Violet Flame will help in the positive growth of any relationship, personal and professional, not just the romantic kind. When relationships come to an end, the Violet Flame can assist closure or can transform and maintain a connection if appropriate.

The Violet Flame works each and every time it is invoked, at atomic level, by transmuting negative energy into positive. It is not necessary for you to understand, or even believe, to get results; the Voilet flame works on the physical, mental and emotional bodies The Voilet Flame will also transmute forgiveness issues, fear, pain, negativity, anger, blame, stress, grief, guilt, anxiety, and anything under the sun.

Here is small decree/ prayer to activate your heart chakra.

Archangel Michael please protect me (3 times)

My heart is the chakra of Violet Fire,

My heart is the purity God desires (3 times)

Focus on the Threefold Flame in the centre of your heart for few seconds and say—

I request Violet Flame to stay with me for the next 24 hours to heal me and balance my relationship with myself and others.

Thank you. Thank you. Thank you

About the Writer

Prathma

Prathma is an expert in various methods of "Wellbeing and Alternative Healing" Modalities. She has been practising & teaching Reiki & other healing Modalities since 1999. A teacher of love and self-acceptance, she brings light and optimism to anyone who meets her. She believes in a holistic approach with a combination and different healing modalities where intuition and logic, science and spirituality go hand-in-hand. Her simplicity and expertise makes the techniques work like powerful charms that have been helping thousands of people around the globe.

VII

Why Are Women Drawn to Bad Boys? Unpacking the Allure and Lessons Learned

Why Are Women Drawn to Bad Boys?

Unpacking the Allure and Lessons Learned

It was one heartbreak after another and I couldn't understand for the life of me why this was happening. Most of my teens went thinking I don't look good or perhaps I'm too fat. When eventually I did manage to lose weight, I thought maybe there was still something wrong with me. Perhaps I talk too much? Or share too much instantly without knowing a person well? Is it the way I talk? Or the way I behave? Am I too nice or not nice enough?

Where exactly was the problem really?

I asked around. I did, I swear. Everyone came up with a different story. For some reason, none of the stories rang true, but then all these stories sounded similar, and it boiled down to one common statement in all of them:

'You have bad taste in men.'

At least if all my friends are saying the same thing, it had to be true, right? So, how is it that these people were experts on who's who and what's what and I wasn't? Was I dumb? Did they have a vetting machine? What was going on and why would nobody tell me? One of the friends said, 'You just know if the other person isn't nice.'

Know how?

Yet another friend said, 'It is kind of obvious. I'm not sure how you don't see it.'

Obvious how?

So if they kind unanimously voted against all the men I have ever dated, it meant everyone should have something in common. So I went on an analysis hunt attempting to find what's common in all these men besides obviously hurting me. It took me months to come back with no answer. I couldn't have avoided any of them even if I knew this 'secret' of what exactly was I missing. I went back to my notes only to realise, having bad taste in men wasn't about me. It was about *them*!

It had always been about *them*! I mean, don't get me wrong. It was about me too but the missing puzzle of the piece was *them*! Here are my findings:

I, like most women on this planet, are made to believe that (trigger warning):

- It's okay if a guy isn't saying nice things to you. Remember that hero from that movie? That's right! He wasn't nice to the actress but look how she forgave him towards the end and they lived happily ever after (on-screen).
- It's okay if someone treats you badly. It is our job as women to forgive. Most movies have that in their story. Some of the parents I know have

that equation too.
- Men who don't treat you well, also known as, ***Bad Boys*** have this "sense of charm", a "charisma"; they reek of adventure...

Hold on! Adventure? Well yeah, obviously until they create trouble in your life, how will you have a story? How will any woman have a happy ending? What will the love story be about? They met, fell in love, got married, had three kids and that's all? Where's the twist? Where's the fun?

That's precisely what ***Bad Boys*** are about. You may try to have fun with them because that's what they're mostly about but if you marry one, boy oh boy (pun intended!) are you in trouble!

I tried doing that. No jokes, personal story.

So, I dated a bad boy and then...

I dated another one.

Did I learn my lesson?

A few years later I did. But here's what happened with one of them. (Nope, not going to tell you which. What's the fun in that?)

So, I fell in love. Hard. We slept together. He never gave me commitment but only asked for being exclusive. I thought, 'hmm. Poor thing! He has been hurt so much in his life. He has commitment issues. But at least we're together and that's what matters.'

A few months into this exclusiveness, I got ghosted. No story, no explanation, no communication. I got an explanation a few weeks later that there were some troubles at his place. Family thing.

We patched up a few months later. Dated for another 2 years. He met my father and then bam! His commitment issues are at the forefront again. He couldn't talk to his parents and tell them about me.

Long story short, I kept hoping for a happy ending. Maybe someday this 'bad boy' will be good and once and for all, I will have a happy ending!

Did I get a happy ending?

Of course, I did!

Was it with him? Hell no!

What did I learn?

Well, heartbreaks or no heartbreaks, I couldn't fall for the potential a person had. He had great potential to be a good partner, but the fact that he couldn't take a stand when it was needed, I couldn't expect anything beyond him later on.

We women love adventures. Don't get me wrong, everyone should have adventures. They're nice getaways to try new things in life- whatever that means for you. But if you find yourself constantly trying to fix things or a person then you, my friend, are dating a bad boy.

RUN!

One of the main things I understood about dating bad boys is that you can't have them for eternity. One way or another you tend to grow out of their tantrums and drama and what then? Well, real life begins where you learn you can no longer keep having the same fights, and same arguments because, unlike the movies, this bad boy ain't learning/improving!

There's only one way out.

Doing what the bad boys do but on your own. Learning how to create that adventure in your own way and try things on your own without "needing" a bad boy or a "prince charming" to rescue you, is a journey worth enjoying once you choose to let them go.

It may be easier said than done for those living in conservative families but if there's one thing I have learned about these situations is that slowly and gradually one tends to find their way out.

am Samara. Maybe even you are. Perhaps we all have been in her place one day or another. Bad boys may be something we all have wanted, dated, experienced and even fantasised about on so many levels, but one thing is clear- they only look good in movies and aren't good for our physical or mental health in real life. There's only so much you as an individual can do about healing them, "fixing them", or even working on them (should you consider them or the relationship as a project), but what if they don't want to be fixed, healed or improved? What then? It's a decision we must make for ourselves.

About the Writer

Arushi Sharma

Arushi is a PhD candidate in Law at Trinity College Dublin and her research work revolves around Data Protection in the financial sector. A full-time law student and a part-time energy worker, she is passionate about teaching and learning. With more than 7 years of experience in healing, she firmly believes in the transformative power of self-reflection and the guidance that each healing offers. Her offerings as a healer and coach help individuals navigate challenges and confidently embrace opportunities.

VIII

Trust, Tacos, and Togetherness: Exploring the Intersection of Food and Connection

Trust, Tacos, and Togetherness:
Exploring the Intersection of Food and Connection

The month of February is often associated with love and relationships, it's an opportune time to reflect on how we can strengthen our connections through the power of food and nutrition. Food is not just sustenance; it's a medium through which we can express care, offer comfort, and foster deeper connections with our loved ones.

Our relationships play a significant role in our mental well-being, whether they are personal or professional. Here are a few things that can help you take care of your mental health as you navigate relationships.

The need for trust – Trust is a cornerstone of any healthy relationship, whether with family, friends, or colleagues.

1. Understanding Your Worth and Value in Relationships

- **Self-reflection:** Reflect on self-worth and establish a solid sense of identity.
- **Boundaries:** Set healthy boundaries in relationships to avoid any emotional distress and maintain self-respect.
- **Empowerment:** Priortize your mental health and understand that you deserve a relationship that nurtures and supports your well-being.

2. Pillars of a Trustworthy Relationship

- **Communication:** It is important to open up and have an honest and clear communication to build trust.
- **Mutual Respect:** It allows both parties to feel valued and heard.
- **Consistency:** It is important to stay consistent with your words and actions, losing which might waver trust.
- **Emotional Safety:** Maintain emotional safety in your relationship where both individuals can be vulnerable and feel supported without any fear of judgement.

3. Cultivating Healthy Relationships that Support Mental Health

- **Choose Quality Over Quantity:** Limit your circle to a few trustworthy people rather than a large group with no support.
- **Emotional Support Networks:** Create a network of friends, family, or mentors who offer genuine emotional support.
- **Conflict Resolution:** Encourage healthy conflict resolution techniques and learn to address disagreements to avoid any misunderstanding and

bitterness.

4. <u>Red Flags in Relationships</u>

- **Toxic Behaviour**: Outline common signs of toxic relationships, such as manipulation, dishonesty, or lack of support.
- **Emotional Drain:** Understand and point out how emotionally draining relationships can impact mental health and self-esteem, leading to stress, anxiety, or depression.
- **Know When to Walk Away**: When a relationship no longer serves their well-being.

5. <u>Nurturing Own Mental Health in Relationships</u>

- **Self-care Practices**: Indulge in self-care and give yourself the love and care you deserve to replenish your mental and emotional energy.
- **Mindfulness and Boundaries:** It is important to be mindful and clear-headed while navigating a complex relationship.
- **Seeking professional Help**: Seeking the help of a professional is important when you are unable to help yourself.

6. <u>Healthy Relationships as a Source of Fulfilment</u>

- **Meaningful Connections**: Building deep, meaningful connections contributes to a sense of purpose and fulfilment in life.
- **Collaboration and Growth:** Seek relationships that encourage personal growth, mutual support, and sharing goals.
- **Joy of Giving and Receiving:** True fulfilment comes from balanced relationships where giving and receiving are mutually beneficial.

The Power of Food in Relationships

- **Sharing meals** is one of the most ancient and enduring social rituals. Whether it's a family dinner, a romantic date, or a casual brunch with friends, the act of eating together fosters a sense of community and belonging. Studies have shown that families who eat together tend to have stronger relationships and better communication.

- **Cooking Together**: Creating memories while cooking together can be a fun and engaging activity that brings people closer. It's an opportunity to learn from each other and create something delicious together.
- **Nourishing Mind and Body**: Nutrition plays a crucial role in mental health. Certain nutrients can reduce anxiety, improve mood, and enhance cognitive function. Omega-3 fatty acids, B vitamins, magnesium, and antioxidants are particularly beneficial.

Recipes

Vegan Tacos With Black Beans and Avocado

Ingredients –
2 Corn Tortillas
½ bowl Balck Beans
1 Avacado
1 Red Cabbage
½ Lime
A pinch of cumin
A pinch of Garlic Powder
A pinch of salt
1 Tbsp olive oil
Method–
Saute the black beans in olive oil along with some cumin, garlic powder, and salt.

To prepare the toppings, slice the avocado and shred the red cabbage.

Now, fill the warm tortillas with the beans & toppings, and in the end, squeeze a lime over it and enjoy!

Salmon and Spinach Salad

Ingredients –
5 Salmon Fillets
20 gm Spinach Leaves

10 gm Cherry Tomatoes
1 Red Onion
4 Walnuts
1 Tbsp Olive Oil
A Pinch of Salt
A pinch of Pepper
Method –
Grill the salmon fillet and set aside.
Mix spinach, cherry tomatoes, red onion, and walnuts in a bowl.
Flake salmon over the salad and dress with olive oil, salt, and pepper.

Recipe for Better Mental Health Management:

Turmeric and Ginger smoothie

Ingredients–
60 ml Almond Milk
1 Banana
Pinch of turmeric
2-inch Ginger
1 Tbsp Honey
1 Tbsp Chia Seeds
Method –
Blend all the ingredients in a blender until smooth.

Dark Chocolate and Walnut Bites

Ingredients–
4 Cubes Dark Chocolate
4 Walnuts
A pinch of salt
Method –
Melt the dark chocolate, and mix the chopped walnuts and spoon onto a baking sheet. Sprinkle salt and refrigerate until set.

Blueberry Oatmeal

Ingredients–
   60 gm Rolled Oats
   60 ml Almond Milk
   10 gm Blueberries
   1 Tbsp Honey
   ½ Tsp Cinamon
   1 Tbsp Chia Seeds
Method –
Cook oats in almond milk and top with blueberries, honey, cinnamon, and chia seeds.

How Hormones, Peer, Surroundings and Mental Health Influence Food Choices

Ghrelin: Known as the hunger hormone, it stimulates appetite. When levels are high, individuals crave high-calorie food.

Leptin: This hormone helps regulate energy balance by inhibiting hunger. High levels signal the brain to reduce appetite. However, leptin resistance can lead to overeating.

Cortisol: Often referred to as the stress hormone, it can increase appetite and cravings for sugary and fatty foods during stressful times.

Insulin: It regulates blood sugar levels. Fluctuation in insulin can influence cravings, particularly carbohydrates.

Estrogen and Progesterone: In women, these hormones fluctuate during the menstrual cycle, affecting appetite and cravings.

Developing a healthy relationship with food is essential for both physical and mental well-being. In today's fast-paced world, our food choices are often influenced by convenience, emotions, and social situations. By understanding these influences and making mindful choices, we can enhance our overall health and happiness.

Understanding Cravings

Cravings are a normal part of life, but they can often lead us to make unhealthy choices. Recognising the difference between physiological and psychological cravings can help manage them better. For example, craving sweets when stressed is common, but opting for a piece of fruit instead of candy can satisfy your cravings and provide valuable nutrition.

Seasonal Foods and Their Benefits

Seasonal food ensures that we get the most nutrient-dense produce available. In winter, root vegetables like carrots and beets are excellent sources of vitamins and minerals that support our immune system.

Navigating Social Situation

Social gatherings often revolve around food, which can make it challenging to stick to healthy choices. One strategy is to practice mindful eating and paying attention to portion size.

Building Self-Control and Healthy Habits

Mindfulness and intuitive eating help us tune into our body signals and make healthier choices. Setting realistic goals like eating a balanced breakfast every day can lead to long-term success. Planning meals can prevent last-minute unhealthy choices.

Practical Tips and Tricks

Swapping unhealthy snacks for nutritious alternatives is a simple way to improve your diet. For example, replace chips with crunchy vegetables and hummus. Keeping a variety of healthy snacks on hand, like nuts and fresh fruits, can manage cravings and keep you satisfied.

About the Writer

Swati Bhutani

With over seven years of experience, Swati Bhutani is a certified dietician known for her expertise in therapeutic diets and weight management. She blends clinical nutrition with Ayurvedic principles to create personalized wellness plans that address individual health needs. Holding a Postgraduate Diploma in Dietetics and Public Health Nutrition from Lady Irwin College and a Fellowship in Clinical Nutrition from Apollo Hospitals, she is skilled in managing conditions like diabetes, cardiovascular health, and hormonal balance. Through a compassionate, sustainable approach, she empowers clients to achieve lasting well-being.

IX

Tarot Predictions for February 2025

Tarot Predictions for
February 2025

Aries (March 21 - April 19): Three of Swords

The Three of Swords for Aries suggests a period of emotional turmoil and disappointment. Past wounds may resurface, leading to feelings of sadness, disappointment, and betrayal.

Career & Finances: There may be unexpected setbacks or delays in your professional endeavours. Avoid impulsive decisions and carefully consider your financial investments.

Love & Relationships: Miscommunication and unresolved conflicts may strain existing relationships. Single Aries may feel disillusioned in their dating lives. Don't wear your heart on your sleeve this month; let your mind also guide you in matters of the heart.

Health: Pay close attention to your mental and emotional well-being. Engage in activities that bring you comfort and solace, such as meditation, yoga, or spending time in nature.

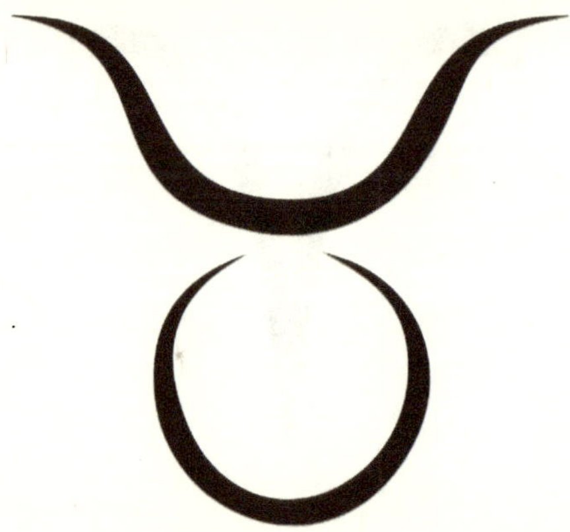

Taurus (April 20 - May 20): Seven of Swords

The Seven of Swords for Taurus indicates a period of deception. This is a time for you to be honest with yourself, at least. don't avoid problems and issues; this is the time to deal with them head-on. At the same time, you need to also use tact to overcome any difficult situations.

Career & Finances: Be wary of hidden agendas and avoid engaging in any shady dealings. Trust your instincts and double-check all agreements before signing on the dotted line. Don't ignore any problems at work, deal with them in a timely manner, no matter how complicated they seem.

Love & Relationships: Communication breakdowns and a lack of trust can create tension in your relationships. Be mindful of your own words and actions, and avoid making assumptions. Clarity and communication are your best friends this month.

Health: Focus on building trust in yourself and your body. Prioritize healthy habits and be mindful of your thoughts and emotions.

Gemini (May 21 - June 20): Queen of Wands

The Queen of Wands for Gemini signifies a period of confidence, creativity, and passion. You'll radiate charisma and possess a magnetic presence. It will be easy for you to manage your personal and professional life with equal ease. Social meetings, get-togethers and networking will be highly rewarding this month.

Career & Finances: This is a good time for pursuing creative projects and taking on leadership roles. Your entrepreneurial spirit will flourish, and financial success is within reach. Promotions are likely to happen soon for you. Keep up your charm and smart work.

Love & Relationships: Your confidence will attract admirers, and existing relationships will deepen and thrive. Embrace your sensuality and enjoy the passionate connections you forge. Your confidence and charisma will attract admirers towards you.

Health: Embrace your inner fire and engage in activities that energize you, such as dancing, hiking, or pursuing a new hobby. Active workouts will benefit you at this time.

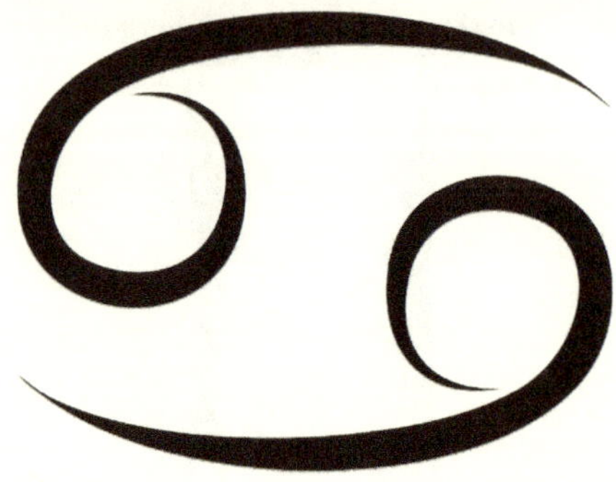

Cancer (June 21 - July 22): Knight of Cups

The Knight of Cups for Cancer suggests a period of romance, creativity, and emotional depth. You'll be guided by your intuition and drawn to experiences that nourish your soul. Emotions will be heightened, causing you to feel hopeful about life around you. At the same time, any low phases are also likely to be felt intensely. Keep your sensitivity protected with gentle energy techniques.

Career & Finances: Your creativity will flow freely, leading to innovative ideas and successful projects. Embrace new opportunities and allow your emotions to guide you towards fulfilling work. You will find your colleagues more open and supportive of your ideas.

Love & Relationships: This is a favourable time for romance and deepening emotional connections. Allow yourself to be vulnerable and open to new experiences. New romances for the singles are possible. Remember not to drown in the deluge of emotional connections and keep your mind sharp as well in matters of the heart.

Health: Nurture your emotional well-being through activities such as art, music, and spending time in nature. Listen to your intuition and prioritise self-care. Health will benefit from emotional healing work.

Leo (July 23 - August 22): Four of Swords

The Four of Swords for Leo suggests a period of rest and recuperation. You may feel the need to retreat from the demands of daily life and recharge your batteries. This period can also serve as a time for going back to the drawing board to check and recheck your plans, where they need changes and plan for the way ahead. When resting the body, remember to rest your mind as well.

Career & Finances: Take a break from the hustle and bustle and focus on prioritising your well-being. Avoid overexerting yourself and delegate tasks whenever possible. This is not the time to take action but to plan ahead and create a roadmap for the future.

Love & Relationships: This is a time for introspection and re-evaluating your relationships. Create space for yourself and allow yourself to reconnect with your inner peace. Don't make any impulsive decisions at this time, as they may backfire.

Health: Prioritize rest and relaxation. Engage in activities that soothe your mind and body, such as meditation, reading, or spending time in nature. Going to a spa and retreat may be a good idea right now.

Virgo (August 23 - September 22): Three of Wands

The Three of Wands for Virgo suggests a period of expansion and new beginnings. You'll be embarking on new adventures and exploring new horizons. This is a time to take stock of your achievements and build ahead. Overall, this is a good month for you to plan ahead. Things are looking up, stay optimistic and get ready to switch gears.

Career & Finances: This is a favourable time for travel, networking, and expanding your horizons. Embrace new opportunities and step outside of your comfort zone. This is not the time to rest or be content. New ambitions will drive you towards fruitful endeavours.

Love & Relationships: You may encounter new and exciting romantic connections. Embrace new experiences and be open to exploring different avenues of love and intimacy. Relationships will be satisfying. If you are single and ready for a relationship, you will meet some good prospects.

Health: Embrace a sense of adventure and explore new ways to enhance your well-being. Engage in activities that invigorate you and expand your horizons.

Libra (September 23 - October 22): Four of Pentacles

The Four of Pentacles for Libra suggests a period of financial stability and security. You'll be focused on building a solid foundation and safeguarding your resources. However, this is not a time to spend your energy, time and resources randomly. Calculated decisions will help you safeguard your energies and fortunes. But remember to keep your heart open in life. Boundaries are good and serve you well, but walls in place of them could harm your relationships.

Career & Finances: This is a good time for financial planning and investing. Focus on building a secure financial future and avoid unnecessary risks. Hold on to your finances and choose to invest wisely.

Love & Relationships: You'll prioritise stability and security in your relationships. Focus on nurturing existing connections and building a strong foundation for the future. Matters of heart cannot be only dealt with by the mind. Have healthy boundaries, but remember to keep the door open as well.

Health: Focus on building healthy habits and creating a sense of stability in your daily routine. Prioritise self-care and ensure you're getting enough rest and nourishment.

Scorpio (October 23 - November 22): The Hanged Man

The Hanged Man for Scorpio suggests a period of introspection and surrender. You may be facing challenges that require you to step back, reassess, and gain a new perspective. Hanged man often comes up when you need to stop and look at the situation from a bird's eye view. What you are looking for is still beyond the horizon, so have patience. Periods of lull are usually periods of preparation. Don't mistake them for a lack of activity because so much is happening underneath the currents of consciousness.

Career & Finances: Unexpected delays or obstacles may arise in your professional endeavours. Embrace this period of pause and use it as an opportunity to reassess your goals and priorities. You might find your finances go through some uncertainties, so make sure you are saving some for the rainy days.

Love & Relationships: Existing relationships may require a period of detachment and introspection. Allow yourself to step back and gain a new perspective on your current situation. stepping back will help you respond instead of reacting to the situation. If you are single, this is a time to evaluate what you are seeking from a relationship and whether you are ready for it.

Health: Embrace periods of stillness and introspection. Engage in activities such as meditation, yoga, or spending time in nature to reconnect with your inner self. This is a good time to go to a retreat centre for some time and space for yourself.

Sagittarius (November 23 - December 21): Ace of Wands

The Ace of Wands for Sagittarius suggests a period of new beginnings and creative inspiration. You'll be brimming with enthusiasm and ready to embark on new adventures. Ace of Wands is all about new opportunities and a burst of energy. Any delays that you may have been experiencing are coming to an end. You will find the energy and opportunity to express your creative potential.

Career & Finances: This is a favourable time for pursuing new projects and embracing new opportunities. Your entrepreneurial spirit will flourish, and success is within reach. Job offers, promotions or a new venture is on the cards for this month. The situation with the finances will soon begin to look up.

Love & Relationships: You'll exude charisma and attract admirers. If you are single, you can experience new romantic connections and allow yourself to be swept away by the excitement of new beginnings.

Health: Embrace your inner fire and engage in activities that energise you. Explore new hobbies, travel to new destinations, and embrace the thrill of new experiences. Any active workouts will help you channel your energies well.

Capricorn (December 22 - January 19): The Fool

The Fool for Capricorn suggests a period of new beginnings and a sense of adventure. You'll be stepping outside of your comfort zone and embracing the unknown. However, this is not the time to blindly jump into something new. Remember to take help and seek advice from experts. You will be well supported in all your ventures. New beginnings are often associated with chaos, so prepare yourself for frantic activity.

Career & Finances: The time is ripe for taking risks and pursuing new opportunities. Embrace the unknown and trust your intuition to guide you towards success. Financially, this period may drain you a bit, so make sure you have something saved to help you through the lean period.

Love & Relationships: New and exciting romantic connections are on the cards. So, if you are single, this is a good time to experience new connections. However, do not be in a hurry to commit. For those in relationships, mind your words, as they may cause unnecessary conflicts.

Health: Embrace a sense of playfulness and spontaneity. Step outside of your comfort zone and explore new ways to enhance your well-being. Adopt that new sport, go for a run or simply pick up a new hobby for better mental health.

Aquarius (January 20 - February 18): The Empress

The Empress for Aquarius suggests a period of nurturing, creativity, and abundance. You'll be radiating warmth and compassion, and your creative energies will flourish. This is a period of abundance, fertility, health and happiness. You will be mentally and emotionally supported. Fortunate experiences will help you make the best of this period.

Career & Finances: This is the right time for nurturing creative projects and building a strong foundation for your future. If you have been planning to start a new venture, the time is ripe now. Embrace your nurturing instincts and create a harmonious and supportive environment.

Love & Relationships: You'll radiate warmth and compassion, attracting love and harmony into your life. Nurture existing relationships and create a loving and supportive environment for your loved ones. This is a good time to plan ahead for the future, whether it is marriage, children or property.

Health: Nurture your body, mind, and soul. Prioritize self-care and engage in activities that bring you joy and fulfilment. Health will support you in every way.

Pisces (February 19 - March 20): Seven of Cups

The Seven of Cups for Pisces suggests a period of indecision and confusion. You may be faced with a multitude of choices and find it difficult to choose the right path. This is also a time when the opportunities need to be checked and rechecked to ensure they are what they seem to be. Your fears may cloud your judgment, so it is a good idea to get help and advice from experts to help you navigate this period.

Career & Finances: Avoid making hasty decisions and take time to carefully consider all your options. The offers may not be as good as they seem to be. Seek guidance from trusted advisors and trust your intuition to guide you towards the right path. Avoid any investments during this period.

Love & Relationships: You may encounter challenges in your relationships due to indecision and a lack of clarity. Take time to reflect on your values and prioritise your own needs. Miscommunications can happen; therefore, avoid assumptions and seek clarity.

Health: Focus on clarifying your intentions and setting clear boundaries. Engage in activities that help you to connect with your inner wisdom and find clarity.

About the writer

Meetu Sehgal

Meetu Sehgal is a Personal Transformation and Emotional Wellness Coach, EFT Trainer, Tarot Reader, Author, Reiki Grandmaster and Counselling Psychologist. With more than 15 years of experience in her field, she has been passionately working with individuals, helping them resolve health, wealth and relationship challenges through coaching. Meetu Sehgal is an MBA graduate from Delhi University and also holds a Masters in Psychology. Passionate about writing and spirituality, she has blended both in her work, which has helped hundreds of people around the world find peace within themselves. Her latest book, "Happy Inside Out", is a definitive guide to understanding and handling emotions and moods.

Spirit Speak

Wisdom through the ages

X

Ancient Wisdom for Modern Living

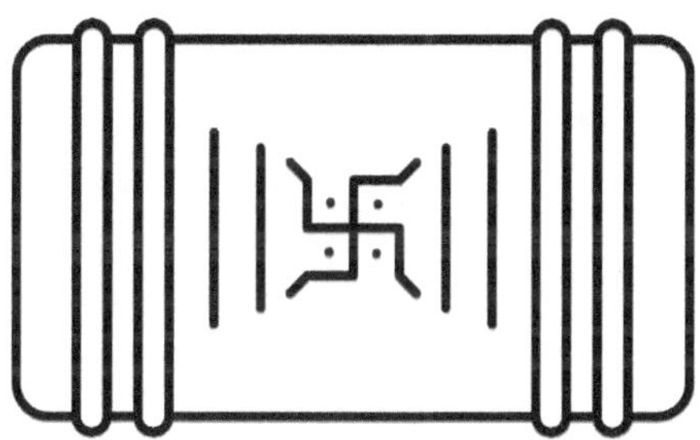

There is a certain reason behind the togetherness of two people,
indeed love is independent of external factors.

XI

The Significance of Namaste

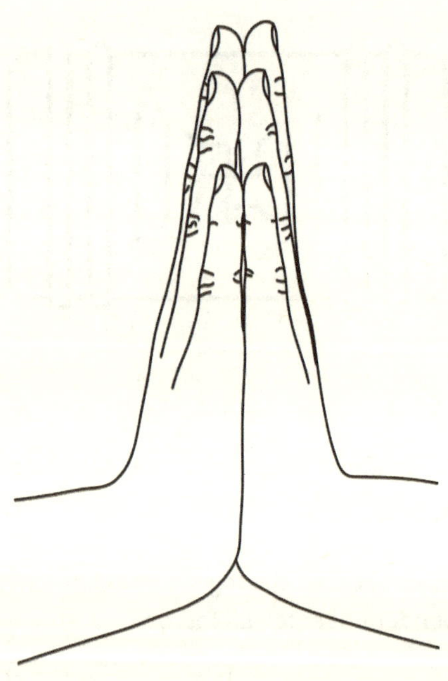

"Namaste" is a traditional Indian greeting that carries deep spiritual and cultural significance. It is derived from Sanskrit, where **"Namaḥ"** means "bow" or "obeisance," and **"Te"** means "to you."

Together, **Namaste** translates to "I bow to you."

Spiritual and Cultural Meaning

1. **Recognition of the Divine** – Namaste is more than just a greeting; it signifies the recognition of the divine spark within each individual. By saying Namaste, one acknowledges, "The divine in me honours the divine in you."
2. **Expression of Respect and Humility** – The gesture of joining palms at the heart (Anjali Mudra) symbolizes humility, gratitude, and deep respect. It is commonly used in spiritual practices, yoga, and meditation.

Symbol of Unity and Harmony – Namaste represents interconnectedness and the idea that all beings are one. It promotes peace, kindness, and understanding in relationships.

XII

Affirmation for the Month

I am open to new, positive connections in my life.
I attract relationships that support my growth and success.
My relationships reflect the love and respect I have for myself.

About Ezine Kaleidoscope

In this new age, the definition and meaning of the word 'Spirituality' has become varied and is often misconstrued with fear, religion and a monk sitting in meditation on a lonely Himalayan mountain.

But spirituality is much beyond this faulty image. It is an inherent part of who we are. Because truly, we are spiritual beings having a human experience.

The purpose of Ezine Kaleidoscope is to bring the true essence of spirituality to our readers and make it so accessible that it doesn't feel like an alien overwhelming concept anymore. Our aim is to make it a part of everyone's everyday life.

If every living moment can be full of awareness, there will be joy and bliss in the world

-Meetu Sehgal

Ezine Kaleidoscope's journey began in November 2010 as a journey towards spirituality, awareness and making the spiritual tools accessible to all in a simple understandable manner.

It is our vision and mission to create awareness and remove the element of fear from spirituality and all things related. It is vested in light and that's what we want to bring to the life of everyone who reads us.

Know more about us

Website: ezinekaleidoscope.com
Email: info@ezinekaleidoscope.com
Instagram: @Ezine.Kaleidoscope
Facebook: www.facebook.com/ezineKaleidoscope

9 798897 240739